christmas drinks

christmas drinks

★

RYLAND
PETERS
& SMALL

LONDON NEW YORK

First published in the USA in 2006 by Ryland Peters & Small, Inc.
519 Broadway, 5th Floor, New York NY 10012
www.rylandpeters.com

10 9 8 7 6 5 4 3 2 1

Text © Maxine Clark, Linda Collister, Tony Conigliaro,
Alice King, Elsa Petersen-Schepelern, Louise Pickford,
Ben Reed, Fran Warde, and Ryland Peters & Small 2006
Design and photographs © Ryland Peters & Small 2006

The recipes in this book have been previously published by
Ryland Peters & Small.

Printed in China.

Library of Congress Cataloging-in-Publication Data

Christmas drinks / Maxine Clark ... [et al.].
    p. cm.
  Includes index.
  ISBN-13: 978-1-84597-296-7
  ISBN-10: 1-84597-296-1
  1. Cocktails. 2. Beverages. 3. Christmas cookery. I. Clark, Maxine.
TX951.C56 2006
641.8'74--dc22
                        2006006986

RECIPE CREDITS **Maxine Clark** page 51; **Linda Collister**
page 52; **Tony Conigliaro** page 35; **Hattie Ellis** page 56;
Alice King page 17; **Elsa Petersen-Schepelern** page 43;
Louise Pickford pages 10, 56; **Ben Reed** pages 9, 10, 13,
14, 17, 18, 21, 22, 25, 27, 28, 31, 32, 35, 36, 39, 40, 41, 44,
48, 55, 59, 60, 62; **Fran Warde** page 47.

conversion chart

Measures have been rounded up or down slightly to make
measuring easier. The key is to keep ingredients in ratio.

Imperial		Metric	
Imperial	1/2 oz.	Metric	10–12.5 ml
	1 oz. (single)		25 ml
	2 oz. (double)		50 ml

contents

From warming cups of mulled wine on Christmas Eve to sparkling glasses of Buck's Fizz on Christmas morning, drinks are an essential part of the festive season. This book features great recipes for every festive gathering, including sophisticated cocktails, nonalcoholic party drinks, and even some life-saving hangover cures for those who've over-indulged a little!

Creating delicious drinks at home doesn't have to be complicated or stressful and with a good selection of spirits, liqueurs, and mixers, you'll have the basic ingredients for most recipes. The only equipment you really need is a cocktail shaker, a barspoon, and a range of different glasses.

If you're catering for a large crowd, make sure that you have plenty of ice in the freezer and offer just a few different drinks so that you don't spend all your time mixing and serving. All of the cocktail recipes serve 1, but if you want to make more, simply multiply the ingredients by the number of drinks you wish to make (a cocktail shaker should hold enough for 3).

Whether it's a festive tipple with old friends or a welcoming mug of hot chocolate when you've come in from the cold weather outside, this collection of recipes will provide all the inspiration you need for a fun and memorable Christmas.

christmas
day brunch

★ bellini

This truly indulgent cocktail makes a delicious treat for Christmas Day brunch. Although there are many variations on this recipe, there is one golden rule for the perfect Bellini—always use fresh, ripe peaches to make the juice.

Purée the peach in a blender and pour into a champagne flute. Pour in the crème de pêche and the peach bitters, if using, then gently top with champagne, stirring carefully and continuously. Garnish with a peach ball in the bottom of the glass, then serve.

½ fresh peach, skinned
½ oz. crème de pêche
a dash of peach bitters (optional)
champagne, to top up
peach ball, to garnish

SERVES **1**

★ campari fizz

1 oz. Campari
½ teaspoon sugar
chilled sparkling wine,
to top up

SERVES 1

This decadent brunchtime drink combines the herby, bitter taste of Campari and the sweetness of sparkling wine with mouthwatering results.

Pour the Campari into a champagne flute and sweeten with the sugar. Top with chilled sparkling wine and serve.

★ mimosa

It is thought that Alfred Hitchcock invented this drink in an old San Francisco eatery called Jack's sometime in the 1940s for a group of friends suffering from hangovers.

½ glass champagne
fresh orange juice, to top up

SERVES 1

Half-fill a champagne flute with champagne. Top with orange juice, stir gently, and serve.

★ kir royale

The epitome of chic sophistication, this simple cocktail will keep everyone happy while the Christmas dinner is cooking.

Add a small dash of crème de cassis to a champagne flute and gently top with champagne. Stir gently and serve.

a dash of crème de cassis
champagne, to top up

SERVES 1

★ champagne julep

This is a good way to use up an opened bottle of bubbly that has lost its fizz as the sugar in the recipe will revitalize it.

To make simple syrup, stir 1 lb. sugar into 1 cup water and bring to a boil, stirring. Cool and keep in a bottle in the refrigerator.

Add the mint, lime juice, and ½ oz. simple syrup to a highball glass filled with crushed ice. Add the champagne (gently) and stir. Garnish with mint.

½ oz. simple syrup (see method)
5 mint sprigs, plus 1 to garnish
a dash of lime juice
champagne, to top up

SERVES 1

★ champagne cocktail

1 white sugar cube
2 dashes of Angostura bitters
1 oz. brandy
dry champagne, to top up

SERVES 1

This classic cocktail has truly stood the test of time, being as popular now as when it was sipped by stars of the silver screen in the 1940s. With a shot of brandy for an extra kick, it is the perfect drink for a Christmas brunch celebration.

Place the sugar cube in a champagne flute and moisten with the Angostura bitters. Add the brandy and stir, then gently top with the champagne and serve.

★ ginger champagne

Ginger and champagne combine perfectly in this delicate and sophisticated cocktail.

Put the ginger in a shaker and press with a barspoon to release the flavor. Add ice and the vodka, then shake and strain into a champagne flute. Top with champagne and serve.

2 thin fresh ginger slices
1 oz. vodka
champagne, to top up

SERVES 1

★ buck's fizz

⅓ glass fresh orange juice
a dash of grenadine (optional)
⅔ glass dry champagne
orange slice (optional), to garnish

SERVES 1

No Christmas morning should be without this classic cocktail which was created by a bartender at Buck's Club, London, in 1921.

Pour the orange juice into a champagne flute, dash with grenadine, if using, and top with chilled champagne. Garnish with an orange slice, if using, then serve.

★ bloody mary

2 oz. vodka
8 oz. tomato juice
2 grinds of black pepper
2 dashes of Worcestershire sauce
2 dashes of Tabasco sauce
2 dashes of fresh lemon juice
1 barspoon horseradish sauce
1 leafy celery stick, to garnish

SERVES 1

Curing hangovers can be painless, and should be enjoyable too. If you can't face the prospect of a champagne cocktail on Christmas morning—or any other morning, for that matter—then this is the answer. You can adjust the measurements according to your likes or dislikes for spices.

Add all the ingredients to a shaker filled with ice. Shake the mixture and strain into a highball glass filled with ice. Garnish with a leafy celery stick and serve.

party cocktails

★ hazelnut martini

This strong, clear martini combines two delicious Christmas treats—chocolate and hazelnut. To decorate the glass, simply wipe the rim with lemon juice, or dip into egg white, then dip into the grated nutmeg.

2 oz. vodka
1 oz. white crème de cacao
2 teaspoons Frangelico
grated nutmeg, for the glass

SERVES 1

Add all the ingredients to a shaker filled with ice. Shake the mixture and strain into a chilled martini glass rimmed with grated nutmeg, then serve.

★ raspberry martini

2 oz. vodka
a dash of crème de framboise
a dash of orange bitters
½ oz. raspberry purée
2 fresh raspberries, to garnish

SERVES 1

This flavored martini is a vibrant red color. It should be quite thick in consistency, so you can replace the purée with a handful of raspberries if you like.

Add all the ingredients to a shaker filled with ice. Shake the mixture and strain into a chilled martini glass. Garnish with two raspberries and serve.

21

★ red star

2 oz. vodka

a bottle of dry vermouth
(Noilly Prat) infused with
1 star anise for 2 days

star anise, to garnish

SERVES 1

This pretty martini is a delicate drink. Ensure
the martini glass is well chilled to highlight
the hint of aniseed.

Pour the vodka and ½ oz. of the star anise-infused
dry vermouth into a mixing glass filled with ice
and stir until the glass is frosted. Strain into a
chilled martini glass and garnish with a star anise.

★ licorice martini

If you're in a rush, pop the licorice into a
bowl of vodka and heat in a microwave
on full power for 2 minutes.

a bottle of vodka infused with
a 4-inch strip of black licorice
for 30 minutes

a dash of Pernod

licorice strip, to garnish

SERVES 1

Pour the vodka into a shaker filled with ice and
shake sharply. Rinse a rocks glass with a dash of
Pernod and discard. Fill the glass with ice, then
strain the mixture into the glass. Garnish with a
strip of licorice and serve.

★ classic cosmopolitan

2 oz. lemon vodka
1 oz. triple sec
1 oz. lime juice
2 oz. cranberry juice

SERVES 1

The TV program *Sex and the City* made this drink popular; its great taste has ensured it stays that way.

Add all the ingredients to a shaker filled with ice. Shake the mixture sharply and strain into a chilled martini glass, then serve.

★ ginger cosmopolitan

2 oz. lemon vodka
1 oz. triple sec
1 oz. fresh lime juice
1 oz. cranberry juice
2 thin ginger slices
flaming orange zest,
to garnish

SERVES 1

Garnishing this gingery cocktail with a flaming orange zest makes a great party trick to impress your guests.

Add all the ingredients to a shaker filled with ice. Shake the mixture sharply and strain into a chilled martini glass. Take a thick(ish) zest from an orange and hold it between your thumb and forefinger, skin down, over the drink. Squeeze the zest so that the oils pass through a naked flame onto the drink's surface. Add the zest, then serve.

★ royal gin fizz

A more sophisticated version of the Gin Fizz—using champagne instead of club soda—this makes the perfect party drink.

Add the egg white, gin, lemon juice, and sugar to a shaker filled with ice. Shake vigorously and strain into a highball glass filled with ice. Top with champagne, garnish with lemon, and serve.

1 egg white
2 oz. gin
1 oz. fresh lemon juice
1 barspoon white sugar or
  ½ oz. simple syrup (page 13)
champagne, to top up
lemon slice, to garnish

SERVES 1

★ sloe gin fizz

1 oz. sloe gin
1 oz. gin
1 oz. fresh lemon juice
½ oz. simple syrup (page 13)
club soda, to top up
lemon slice, to garnish

SERVES 1

Sloe gin is a sweet liqueur traditionally made in the fall and drunk at Christmas. Commercial brands vary considerably so you may need to adjust the measurements.

Add all the ingredients to a shaker filled with ice. Shake sharply and strain the mixture into a highball glass filled with ice. Top with club soda, garnish with lemon, and serve with two straws.

★ sour italian

1 oz. Campari
½ oz. Strega
½ oz. Galliano
1 oz. fresh lemon juice
½ oz. cranberry juice
½ oz. simple syrup (page 13)
a dash of egg white
2 dashes of Angostura bitters

SERVES 1

This cocktail is made with completely Italian ingredients and the colors look wonderfully festive. If a fruitier cocktail is more to your taste, wipe some orange zest around the top of the glass and add some to the drink.

Add all the ingredients to a shaker filled with ice. Shake the mixture and strain into a wine glass or a champagne flute, then serve.

★ boston sour

This classic sour is usually made with Scotch whiskey, but using bourbon instead adds a little vanillary sweetness.

Add all the ingredients to a shaker filled with ice. Shake the mixture sharply and strain into a whiskey tumbler filled with ice. Garnish with a lemon slice and a maraschino cherry and serve.

2 oz. bourbon
1 oz. fresh lemon juice
2 barspoons simple syrup (page 13)
2 dashes of Angostura bitters
a dash of egg white
lemon slice and maraschino cherry, to garnish

SERVES 1

★ sidecar

The pretty sugar frosting on the glass is easy
to achieve. Simply wipe the rim of the glass
with lemon juice, or dip into egg white,
then dip into a small dish of sugar.

Add all the ingredients to a shaker filled with ice.
Shake the mixture and strain into a chilled martini
glass with a sugared rim, then serve.

2 oz. brandy
1 oz. fresh lemon juice
1 oz. Cointreau
sugar, for the glass

SERVES 1

★ triple gold margarita

2 oz. gold tequila
½ oz. Cointreau
½ oz. Grand Marnier
1 oz. fresh lime juice
1 oz. Goldschlager

SERVES 1

This cocktail will bring a touch of splendor
to any Christmas party. It is layered with a
float of Goldschlager, a cinnamon-flavored
liqueur laced with real 24 carat gold pieces.

Add all the ingredients, except the Goldschlager,
to a shaker filled with ice. Shake the mixture
sharply and strain into a chilled margarita glass.
Float the Goldschlager onto the surface and serve.

★ turkish chocolate

2 oz. vodka
½ oz. white crème de cacao
2 dashes of rose water
cocoa powder, for the glass

SERVES 1

This rich cocktail makes a truly delightful Christmas treat. To decorate the glass, wipe the rim with lemon juice, or dip into egg white, then dip into the cocoa powder.

Add all the ingredients to a shaker filled with ice. Shake the mixture and strain into a chilled martini glass rimmed with cocoa powder, then serve.

★ silk stocking

If you're too old to receive a stocking full of gifts at Christmas, then this smooth tequila cocktail will make a more than adequate substitute.

Put all the ingredients in a blender. Add two scoops of crushed ice and blend for 20 seconds. Pour the mixture into a hurricane glass, garnish with two raspberries, and serve with two straws.

1½ oz. gold tequila
½ oz. white crème de cacao
1 teaspoon grenadine
½ oz. heavy cream
2 fresh raspberries, to garnish

SERVES 1

★ the twinkle

Combining vodka with another indulgence, champagne, and the enigmatic flavor of elderflower gives a sparkling result.

Stir the ingredients over ice in a mixing glass, then strain into a martini glass. Garnish with a twist of lemon and serve.

2 oz. vodka
1 oz. champagne
a dash of elderflower cordial
lemon twist, to garnish

SERVES 1

★ moscow mule

2 oz. vodka
½ lime, cut into four wedges
ginger beer, to top up

SERVES 1

This refreshing cocktail is easy to make and is ideal for serving at a big Christmas gathering. The ginger beer gives it a real kick and a lovely spiciness.

Pour the into a highball filled with ice. Squeeze the lime into the glass. Top with ginger beer and stir with a barspoon. Serve with a straw.

★ black velvet

½ glass Guinness
champagne, to top up

SERVES **1**

This one of the most tempting and drinkable
cocktails. Pour gently into the glass to allow
for the unpredictable nature of both the
Guinness and the champagne.

Half-fill a champagne flute with Guinness, gently
top with champagne, and serve.

★ perfect manhattan

"Perfect" does not refer to how well this
whiskey-based cocktail is put together, but
the perfect balance between sweet and dry.

Ensure that the ingredients are very cold and add
them to a mixing glass filled with ice. Stir the
mixture until chilled. Strain into a chilled martini
glass, garnish with a strip of lemon, and serve.

2 oz. rye whiskey
½ oz. sweet vermouth
½ oz. dry vermouth
a dash of Angostura bitters
lemon strip, to garnish

SERVES **1**

nonalcoholic
drinks

★ virgin mary

If you can't face alcohol, this nonalcoholic version of a Bloody Mary (page 18) is the solution. You may want to add extra spices to compensate for the lack of vodka.

Add all the ingredients to a shaker filled with ice. Shake the mixture and strain into a highball glass filled with ice. Garnish with a celery stick, if liked.

10 oz. tomato juice
2 grinds of black pepper
2 dashes of Tabasco sauce
2 dashes of Worcestershire sauce
2 dashes of fresh lemon juice
1 barspoon horseradish sauce
celery stick, to garnish (optional)

SERVES 1

★ shirley temple

1 oz. grenadine
ginger ale or lemon soda,
to top up
lemon slice, to garnish

SERVES 1

A thirst-quencher for those with a very sweet-tooth named, most appropriately, after the famous Hollywood child actress.

Pour the grenadine into a highball glass filled with ice and top with ginger ale or lemon soda. Garnish with lemon and serve with a straw.

1 oz. concentrated
   fruit syrup
   (of your choice)
club soda or
   sparkling water,
   to top up
a garnish of your choice

SERVES 1

★ squash highball

This simple drink makes a refreshing change
from orange juice if you're avoiding alcohol.
Serve with a garnish that suits the flavor of
your chosen fruit syrup.

Pour the fruit syrup into a highball glass filled with
ice and top with club soda or sparkling water.
Serve with your chosen garnish.

5 oz. fresh orange juice
5 oz. fresh grapefruit juice
a dash of grenadine
2 dashes of fresh lemon juice

SERVES 1

★ pussy foot

Even nonalcoholic cocktails should aim
for the perfect contrast of sweet and sour
flavors. Try using fresh pineapple juice
instead of grapefruit for a sweeter version.

Add all the ingredients to a shaker filled with
ice. Shake the mixture and strain into a highball
glass filled with ice, then serve.

★ ginger beer

A great party drink for kids and adults alike, this recipe is quick to make and has a delicious fresh taste. Ginger beer is also good for calming upset stomachs and soothing indigestion, coughs, and colds. Don't peel the ginger if you're blending it in a food processor—just chop it up coarsely, then pulse until well chopped. The skin will give the beer extra flavor.

Put all the ingredients into a large French press or heatproof pitcher. Pour over 1 quart boiling water, and stir until the sugar dissolves.

Cool, plunge or strain, then chill well. To serve, half-fill glasses with the mixture and top with club soda or sparkling water.

4 oz. grated fresh ginger
zest and juice of 2 limes
2 cloves
1 cup sugar, preferably brown
club soda or sparkling water, to top up

SERVES 4

★ liver recovery

2 green apples
1 banana
6 fresh strawberries

SERVES 1

This tasty combination of strawberry, banana, and apple is packed with nutrients. It contains all the necessary goodness to restore an ailing liver without having to resort to milk thistle pills.

Peel, core, top, and tail the assembled fruits, as necessary. Put each of them through a juicer, then add the juices to a blender filled with a scoop of crushed ice. Blend and pour into a small highball glass, then serve.

winter
warmers

★ mulled wine

Warm your house and make your friends' hearts glow with this traditional winter drink, also known as *glühwein*. If you are making it for a big party, simply add more wine and sugar to the pan during the evening.

Pour the red wine into a large saucepan. Insert the cloves into the orange peel, then cut the oranges into quarters.

Add the orange pieces to the pan with the sugar, ginger, cinnamon, and nutmeg. Heat the mixture to simmering point and simmer for 8–10 minutes. Serve hot in goblets or wine glasses, distributing the pieces of orange among the glasses.

2 bottles red wine, 750 ml each

8 cloves

2 oranges

3 tablespoons brown sugar

2 inches fresh ginger, peeled and chopped

1 cinnamon stick

½ teaspoon grated nutmeg

SERVES 4

★ hot toddy

5 cloves
2 lemon slices
2 oz. whiskey
1 oz. fresh lemon juice
2 barspoons honey
3 oz. hot water
1 cinnamon stick

SERVES 1

With its warming blend of spices and sweet honey aroma, this is the perfect comforter and will soothe any aches, snuffles, or alcohol withdrawal symptoms.

Skewer the cloves into the lemon slices and add them to a heatproof glass or a toddy glass along with the rest of the ingredients, then serve.

★ blue blazer

This spectacular drink is best practised in the confines of the kitchen before attempting to make it in front of an audience.

Warm two small metal tankards. In one, dissolve the sugar in the water. Pour the whiskey into the other, set alight and, as it burns, pour it into the first tumbler and back, creating a continuous stream of fire. Once the flame has subsided, pour it into a warmed glass and garnish with nutmeg.

1 sugar cube
2 oz. boiling water
2 oz. whiskey
grated nutmeg, to garnish

SERVES 1

★ glögg

This comforting, heart-warming drink is served in cafés in Denmark and Sweden to cheer up bleak winter days. It has a miraculous effect.

Pour 1 bottle of red wine into a nonreactive bowl or saucepan. Add the sugar, raisins, and almonds and stir to dissolve the sugar. Put the spices in a cheesecloth bag, tie with string, and add to the wine. Leave to infuse for 2 hours if possible.

Heat the wine until almost boiling, then cover and leave to infuse for at least 30 minutes (you can also do this in the morning if serving it at night). When ready, remove the spice bag and pour in the remaining bottle of wine, the schnapps, and brandy. Reheat until almost boiling and serve hot in glass cups with spoons to eat the raisins and almonds.

2 bottles medium red wine, 750 ml each

⅔ cup sugar

1–1½ cups mixed raisins and slivered almonds

1 cinnamon stick

4 cloves

8 cardamom pods, lightly crushed

1-inch piece of fresh ginger, lightly smashed

¾ cup schnapps or vodka

½ cup brandy or cognac

a cheesecloth bag
kitchen twine

SERVES 8

★ finest hot chocolate

3 oz. plain chocolate,
broken into pieces
1 tablespoon sugar, or to taste
1 vanilla pod, split lengthwise
1¾ cups milk
⅓ cup heavy cream, whipped
freshly grated chocolate or cocoa
powder, for sprinkling

SERVES 2

The ultimate hot drink—the best quality
chocolate, a hint of vanilla, lots of frothy
milk topped with whipped cream and
grated chocolate. Make sure the mugs
or cups are warmed beforehand.

Put the chocolate pieces, sugar, vanilla pod, and
milk into a small, heavy saucepan. Heat gently,
stirring, until the chocolate has melted, then
bring to a boil, whisking constantly with a
balloon whisk, until very smooth and frothy.
Remove the vanilla pod.

Pour into warmed mugs, top with whipped
cream and a sprinkling of freshly grated
chocolate or cocoa, and serve immediately.

★ irish coffee

The trick to this great *digestif* is not to go crazy with the cream. Sweetening the coffee does help the cream sit well, but if you don't take sugar it should still work.

Mix the whiskey and simple syrup in a heatproof glass and add coffee to taste, making sure it is piping hot. Gently layer the cream over the surface of the coffee, using a flat-bottomed barspoon or a teaspoon. Garnish with coffee beans and serve.

1½ oz. Irish whiskey
½ oz. simple syrup (page 13)
8 oz. heavy cream
double espresso, to taste
3 coffee beans, to garnish

SERVES 1

★ mudslide

1 oz. vodka
1 oz. Bailey's
1 oz. Kahlúa
1 oz. heavy cream (optional)
cocoa powder, to garnish

SERVES 1

With the added kick of the vodka, this warming drink will both caress your taste buds and lure you onto slippery slopes.

Add all the ingredients to a shaker filled with ice. Shake sharply and strain into a rocks glass filled with ice. Alternatively, mix in a blender with crushed ice for 10 seconds. Garnish and serve.

★ ginger & lemon tisane

2 inches fresh ginger, peeled
2 stalks lemongrass
4 teaspoons honey
4 lemon slices
boiling water, to top up

SERVES 4

This lightly spiced tisane has a wonderful cleansing effect on the body, making an ideal start to a cold winter's day.

Thinly slice the ginger and cut each lemongrass stalk in half crosswise, then lengthwise, then divide among four cups. Add the honey and lemon slices. Top with boiling water and serve.

★ chai masala

This delicious spiced Indian tea is good for warding off colds. If making a larger quantity, use dried ginger instead of fresh and mix the spices well before using.

Put 1 cup water with the milk and sugar in a saucepan. Add the tea and spices. Bring to a boil, reduce the heat, and simmer for 2 minutes. Strain into small cups and serve.

½ cup milk
2 teaspoons sugar
1 teaspoon black tea
¼ teaspoon ground nutmeg
¼ teaspoon finely grated ginger
3 cloves
seeds of 3 green cardamom pods
a pinch of ground cinnamon

SERVES 2

after-dinner cocktails

★ brandy alexander

The Brandy Alexander is the perfect after-dinner cocktail—luscious, seductive, and great for chocolate lovers. It is important to get the proportions just right so that the brandy stands out as the main flavor.

Add all the ingredients to a shaker filled with ice. Shake and strain into a chilled martini glass. Garnish with grated nutmeg and serve.

2 oz. brandy
½ oz. brown or white
  crème de cacao
½ oz. heavy cream
grated nutmeg, to garnish

.

SERVES 1

★ stinger

2 oz. brandy
1 oz. white crème de menthe

SERVES 1

A great palate cleanser and *digestif* which, like brandy, should be consumed after dinner. The amount of crème de menthe used depends on personal taste: too much and the result is akin to liquid toothpaste.

Add all the ingredients to a shaker filled with ice. Shake and strain into a chilled martini glass.

★ silver streak

1 oz. chilled vodka
1 oz. chilled kummel

SERVES 1

Kummel is one of the least frequently used liqueurs in cocktails, more's the pity. It has a distinctive, almost aniseedlike taste that comes from the caraway seeds used in its production, and as an added bonus it promotes good digestion. For best results keep both the vodka and the kummel in a refrigerator or freezer and pour them gently into a sturdy rocks glass.

Pour the chilled vodka into a rocks glass filled with ice. Pour in the chilled kummel, then stir gently and serve.

★ black russian

2 oz. vodka
1 oz. Kahlúa

SERVES 1

The Black and White Russians are classics that have been around for many years. The sweet coffee flavor of the Kahlúa is sharpened by the vodka to create these stylish after-dinner cocktails.

Add the vodka and Kahlúa to a shaker filled with ice. Shake the mixture and strain into a rocks glass filled with ice, then serve.

★ white russian

The White Russian, with its addition of the cream float, makes the perfect nightcap.

2 oz. vodka
1 oz. Kahlúa
1 oz. cream
maraschino cherry, to garnish

SERVES 1

Add the vodka and Kahlúa to a shaker filled with ice. Shake and strain into a rocks glass filled with ice, then gently layer on the cream over the back of a barspoon. Garnish with a maraschino cherry and serve.

★ index

PHOTOGRAPHY CREDITS All photographs by **William Lingwood** except the following: **Debi Treloar** Pages 19, 46; **Ian Wallace** Pages 11, 57; **Martin Brigdale** Page 53; **James Merrell** Page 42; **Noel Murphy** Page 50